THIS BOOK BELONGS TO:

. . . .

. . . .

. . . .

. . . .

. . . .

. . . .

OTHER BOOKS YOU MAY LIKE

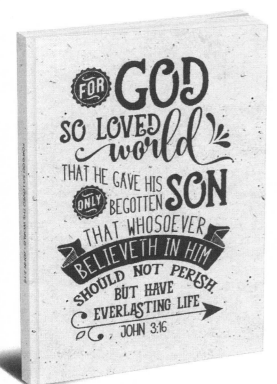

All Things Are Possible
Mark 9:23
(8 x 10) (Dot Grid)
Blank Journal

https://www.amazon.com/dp/1092640142

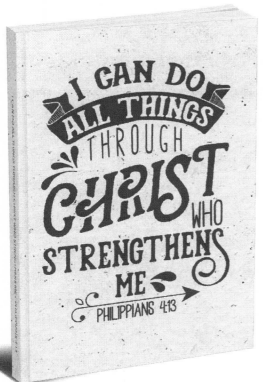

I Can Do All Things
Philippians 4:13
(8 x 10) (Dot Grid)
Blank Journal

https://www.amazon.com/dp/172029819X

Hello,

Thank you for purchasing this book. We hope you have enjoyed using it as much as we enjoyed designing it. We are a small husband and wife business. Words cannot express how much we appreciate that you bought our book.

It would help us a lot if you could take a moment and leave a review about this book on Amazon.

Thanks again, Belle Journals

8 X 10 DOT GRID

LEAVE A REVIEW BUY IT AGAIN

All Things Are Possible
Mark 9:23
(8 x 10)(Dot Grid)
Blank Journal

https://www.amazon.com/dp/1721827587

Made in the USA
Monee, IL
06 May 2022

95962093R00072